How LOVING God Must Be!

Written by: Jessica Smith
Illustrated by: Ryan Gillum and Scrappy Miller

Published by
Carpe Diem Publishers
P.O. Box 2146
San Benito, TX 78586
806-433-6321

www.carpediempublishers.com
How LOVING God Must Be!
Copyright© 2020 by Jessica Smith
All Rights Reserved
No portion of this book may be reproduced, stored in a retrieval system, or transmitted, in any form or by any means, eletronic, mechanical, photocopying, recording, or otherwise without prior written permission from the publisher.

Printed in the United States of America
ISBN: 978-1-949215-10-6

To my wonderful kids -
Nathan, Nelle and Callum

I hope all three of you spend your whole lives understanding how LOVING, KIND and GENTLE God is. He loves you all more than you will ever know. Love him back with all your heart, soul, mind and strength! And raise your babies to love God the same!

Love,
Mom

A mother holds her newborn baby closely to her chest and smiles.

How **JOYFUL** God must be!

The leaves of tall trees cheer loudly as a cool wind flies through them.

How **PEACEFUL** God must be!

A raging storm on a large ocean quickly turns soft and still.

How **CALM** God must be!

An owl stands on the highest stone on the highest mountain and looks out over the green waves.

How **WONDERFUL** God must be!

A squirrel gathers nuts for the approaching winter.

How **WISE** God must be!

Our magnificent sun shines high in the sky.

How **BRIGHT** God must be!

An old man leaves the last cookie for the little youngster in-line behind him.

How **KIND** God must be!

A sweet girl nurses her baby goat back to health.

How **GENTLE** God must be!

A father runs into a burning house to save his little child.

How **BRAVE** God must be!

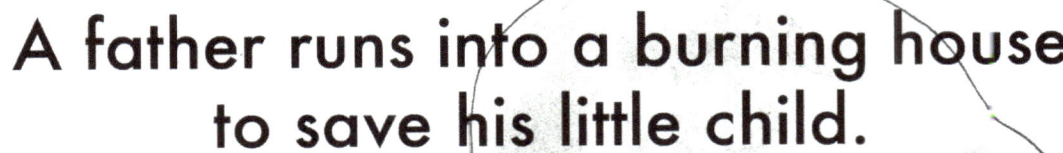

An asteroid zooms past a planet and continues exploring the endless universe.

How **WONDROUS** God must be!

Flowers go to sleep every winter and re-awaken every spring.

How **FAITHFUL** God must be!

A young boy gives a fresh flower and his drawing of clouds to his mother.

How **PURE** God must be!

A mighty wind pushes a cloud across a nation.

How **STRONG** God must be!

God's hands guard our souls.

How **CHIVALROUS** God must be!

The Father allowed His Son to save the people of the earth.

How **LOVING** God must be!

www.ingramcontent.com/pod-product-compliance
Lightning Source LLC
Chambersburg PA
CBHW041220240426
43661CB00012B/1101